A PICTURE BOOK OF JEWISH HOLIDAYS

by David A. Adler
illustrated by Linda Heller

Holiday House, New York

Library of Congress Cataloging in Publication Data

Adler, David A.
A picture book of Jewish holidays.

Summary: Highlights the Sabbath, Rosh Hashanah,
Yom Kippur, Sukkot, Simhat Torah, Hanukkah, Tu bi-
Shevat, Purim, Passover, Yom ha-Azma'ut, Shavuot,
Tishah be-Av, and other Jewish holidays.
1. Fasts and feasts—Judaism—Pictorial works—
Juvenile literature.   [1. Fasts and feasts—Judaism]
I. Heller, Linda.   II. Title.
BM690.A38   296.4'3   81-2765
ISBN 0-8234-0396-3   AACR2

To Nathan, Rachel,
Noam, and Ari

D.A.

To Rose

L.H.

CONTENTS

The Jewish calendar is based on the moon
and has been used for more than 5,000 years.
Jewish holidays are celebrated on the same dates each year
on the Jewish calendar.
But the dates on the newer Julian calendar,
which is based on the sun,
change from year to year.
This drawing shows the two calendars together.

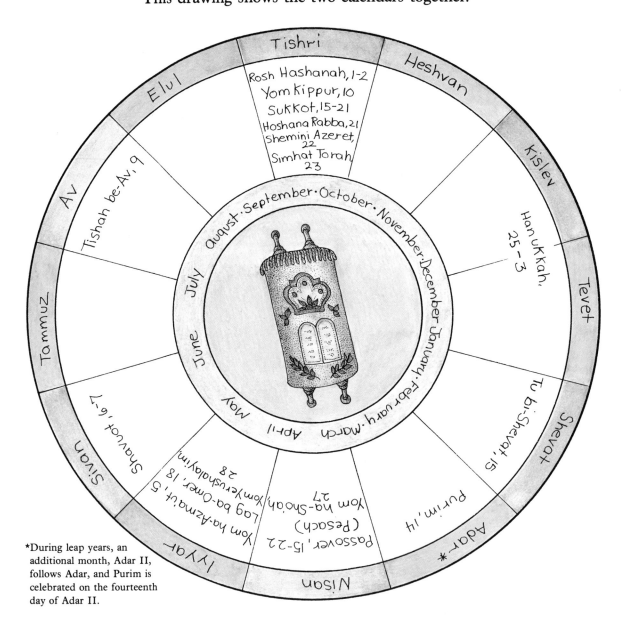

Tishri

Rosh Hashanah, 1-2
Yom Kippur, 10
Sukkot, 15-21
Hoshana Rabba, 21
Shemini Azeret, 22
Simhat Torah, 23

Heshvan

Elul

Kislev

Hanukkah, 25-3

Av

Tishah be-Av, 9

Tevet

August · September · October · November · December · January · February · March

July

June

May

April

Tammuz

Tu bi-Shevat, 15

Shevat

Sivan

Shavuot, 6-7

Adar*

Purim, 14

Iyyar

Yom ha-Azma'ut, 5
Lag ba-Omer, 18
Yom Yerushalayim, 28

Yom ha-Sho'ah, 27

Passover, 15-22
(Pesach)

Nisan

*During leap years, an
additional month, Adar II,
follows Adar, and Purim is
celebrated on the fourteenth
day of Adar II.

This is not a book of facts
but of feelings.
It's filled with the warmth of the Sabbath,
the solemnity of Yom Kippur,
the wonder of Hanukkah,
the joy of Purim,
the awe of Shavuot,
and more.
It's filled with the love Jewish people
have for their traditions and holidays.

THE SABBATH

At the end of each week,
as the sun sets on Friday,
we light candles in our homes
to welcome the Sabbath.

The Sabbath is the day of rest.
It is the day God rested
after six days of creation.
It is the day we rest
after six days of work.

On the Sabbath
parents bless their children.
Kiddush is said—a blessing over wine.
We go with our families to a synagogue or temple
where the Torah is read.
We sing. We rest.
We enjoy the day and each other.

It is said,
that for Jews,
the Sabbath has
the sweet taste of Heaven.

ROSH HASHANAH

Some rabbis say that in Heaven
God keeps a book for us.
In the book God writes
all the good things we do,
and the bad things too.
On Rosh Hashanah, the Jewish New Year,
God opens the book.
He looks at what we've done
and decides
whether we'll have a good year
or a bad one,
and whether we'll be happy or not.

On Rosh Hashanah,
in synagogues and temples,
we pray that in the year ahead
God will be good to us.
We also hear the sounds of the shofar—ram's horn.
Those sounds remind us to obey God's laws
and to be good to others.

YOM KIPPUR

Yom Kippur is also called
the Day of Atonement. It is a fast day.
Adults do not eat or drink.
We think about what we have done wrong
in the old year,
and we ask God to forgive us.
We ask the people we have sinned against
to forgive us too.
We think about how we can be better
in the year ahead
and we pray to God.

We pray for a year
of happiness and good health.
We pray for a year of peace
for us,
our families,
our friends,
our neighbors
and the world.

SUKKOT

A sukkah is a booth
with a roof made of branches.
If you sit in a sukkah,
you can look through the roof
and see the sky.
The sukkot we sit in
during the holiday of Sukkot
remind us of the booths the Jews lived in
when they wandered in the desert
before they came to Israel.

In synagogues and temples,
we also wave and hold together
an etrog, lulav, aravot, and hadassim,
the fruit and branches
of four very different trees.

Some rabbis say this teaches us
that for real happiness
all the different people of the world
must work together in peace.

SIMHAT TORAH

"Let's sing!
Let's dance!
It's Simhat Torah!"

Simhat Torah is the day
the reading of the Torah
is completed in the synagogue.
It's also the day
the reading of the Torah
begins all over again.
You see,
we can never be finished
reading and studying the Torah.
There is always more we can learn.

HANUKKAH

Hanukkah is a holiday of miracles.
The miracles happened over 2,000 years ago.
A powerful king robbed and spoiled the Jewish Temple.
He tried to force the Jews
to give up their religion.
He couldn't.
A small band of Jews
fought against the king's huge army
and won.

The Temple was cleaned,
and the people wanted to light the menorah.
But only one small jar
of pure oil was found.
It would take eight days
to prepare more.

The menorah was lit
and the oil in that one small jar
burned and burned
until more oil could be prepared.

Today, we light candles
on each of the eight nights of Hanukkah.
We remember those few brave Jews
who fought a whole army
and won.
And we remember the small jar of oil
that burned for so long.

TU BI-SHEVAT

In Israel and all over the world,
trees are important.
People eat their fruit
and use their wood for building.
A tree's roots keep the soil
from being washed away by the rain.
And, because trees are so important,
they have their own holiday.
It's called Tu bi-Shevat.

On Tu bi-Shevat
we eat figs, dates, oranges, carob,
apricots, almonds, raisins, grapefruits,
and many of the other fruits
which grow in Israel.

On Tu bi-Shevat in Israel,
children plant trees,
and, as the children grow
bigger, taller and stronger,
so do the trees.

PURIM

In ancient Persia
a man named Haman
tried to destroy the Jewish people.
He didn't.
The Jews were saved by Queen Esther
and her cousin Mordecai.
That's part of the story of Purim.
The whole story is in the Megillah,
a scroll that's read on Purim.
And as the Megillah is read,
children listen.
When they hear the name
of the wicked Haman,
they yell "Hiss!" and "Boo!"
They stomp their feet
and shake gragers, Purim noisemakers.
After all,
why should the happy holiday of Purim
be spoiled
by hearing the name
of such a wicked man?

PASSOVER (PESACH)

Freedom—it's wonderful.
It's why we celebrate Passover.
We celebrate with a special "seder" meal.
At the seder we remember the time
the Jews were slaves in Egypt.
At the seder we eat matzah,
a flat kind of bread.
It reminds us
that the Jews left Egypt so quickly,
the bread they were baking
didn't have a chance to rise.
The herbs we eat at the seder
are bitter
and so was slavery.
The four cups of wine we drink
are sweet,
but the freedom we enjoy
has the sweetest taste of all.

YOM HA-AZMA'UT

Do miracles still happen?
Sure they do!
In 1948,
after almost 2000 years
of being chased from one country
to another,
the Jews had a land of their own.
They called it Israel.
Thousands of people
worked and fought to make that miracle happen.
And today,
millions celebrate
and march in parades
on Yom ha-Azma'ut, Israel's Independence Day.

SHAVUOT

Shavuot is the anniversary of the day
God gave us the Torah.
It was a day filled with wonder and awe.
The whole Jewish people
gathered around a mountain, Mount Sinai.
Smoke covered the top of the mountain.
Then thunder roared and lightning flashed.
A trumpet sounded. The people trembled.
The mountain itself shook.
A voice called out,
"I am the Lord, your God.
It was I who brought you out of slavery.
You shall have no other god but Me."
And God gave the people His Ten Commandments.
Then Moses climbed the mountain
and God gave him His greatest gift,
the Torah.
When Moses climbed down the mountain,
he taught the Torah to all the people of Israel.

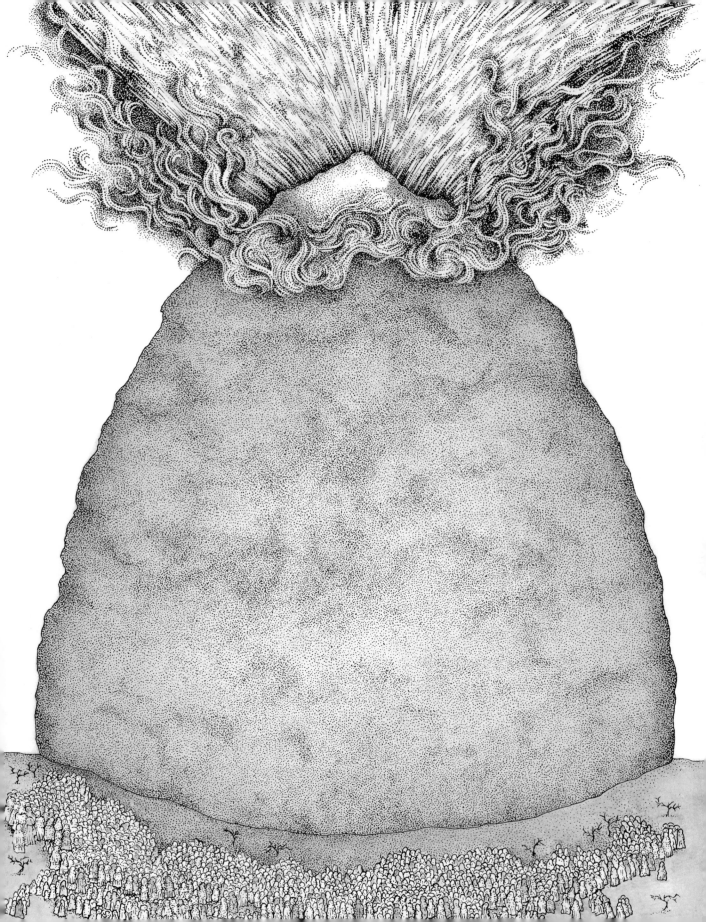

TISHAH BE-AV

Tishah be-Av is a day for remembering.
We remember many of the terrible things
that have happened to the Jews.
We remember when the first
and second Temples were destroyed.
We remember the great Jewish scholars
who were tortured and killed.

On Tishah be-Av
we sit on hard benches.
We don't wear comfortable shoes.
Adults do not eat or drink.
In some synagogues, the Torah and Ark
are draped in black.
Tishah be-Av is a very sad day.

OTHER HOLIDAYS

ROSH HODESH is the first day and sometimes the first two days of each month in the Jewish calendar.

On HOSHANA RABBA, the seventh day of Sukkot, we carry the lulav and etrog and make seven circuits around the synagogue. We also say special prayers because this is the day the judgments of Rosh Hashanah and Yom Kippur become final.

SHEMINI AZERET is the day after Hoshana Rabba and the day the prayer for rain is said.

YOM HA-SHO'AH is also called "The Holocaust and Ghetto Remembrance Day." It's the day set aside to remember all the Jews who were murdered not so long ago in Europe.

LAG BA-OMER is the one day during the Omer, the weeks between Passover and Shavuot, when there are celebrations. That's because, many years ago, there was a plague that killed young Jewish scholars on all but one day of the Omer—Lag ba-Omer.

YOM YERUSHALAYIM celebrates the day the old city and the new city of Jerusalem were united and Jews could once again visit the Western Wall of the ancient Jewish Temple.

GLOSSARY

ARAVOT—branches from a willow tree.

ARK—cabinet in the synagogue containing the Torah scrolls.

ETROG—citron, a certain fruit in the citrus—orange and grapefruit—family.

HADASSIM—branches from a myrtle bush.

LULAV—palm branch.

MATZAH—bread which has not been given a chance to rise.

MENORAH—lamp in the Temple which held seven lights. Menorah also often refers to the Hanukkah lamp which holds eight regular lights and one extra light, the *shammash.*

RABBI—Hebrew for "my master"; a Jewish religious leader or teacher.

SEDER—traditional Passover meal.

SYNAGOGUE, TEMPLE—Jewish houses of prayer. Temple also refers to the two ancient Temples of Jerusalem.

TEN COMMANDMENTS—basic laws announced by God at Mount Sinai.

TORAH—The first five books of the Bible, also called The Five Books of Moses or The Law.